Millionaire Mindset

Millionaire Mindset

Transforming Your Wealth from the Inside Out

B. Vincent

QuillQuest Publishers

Contents

Chapter 1: Introduction to the Millionaire Mindset

Figuring out the brain research of abundance

Chasing after monetary achievement, it is important to dive into the complicated brain science that supports abundance aggregation. This part disentangles the mysterious attitude that distinguishes tycoons from the rest, revealing insight into the significant rules that oversee their monetary excursion. By exposing unavoidable fantasies encompassing riches and achievement, perusers are welcome to reevaluate their points of view, opening their brains to the endless conceivable outcomes that lie ahead. We leave on a groundbreaking investigation of the idea of an overflow mindset—aa philosophy that rises above simple material procurement, including a comprehensive point of view's overflow. Through reflection and disclosure, perusers are directed to perceive the influence inherent in taking on an overflow outlook, making way for a significant change in their relationship with riches. Drawing from mental examination and genuine accounts, this segment enlightens the significant impact of conviction frameworks on one's monetary reality. By analyzing the multifaceted interchange between considerations, convictions, and activities, perusers are enabled to distinguish and conquer the restricting convictions that might have until recently obstructed their monetary development. Equipped with recently discovered mindfulness, they are ready to develop a mentality established in probability and overflow—an outlook that fills in as the foundation of persevering through monetary achievement.

The Force of Conviction Frameworks

Inside the unpredictable embroidery of our brains lies the significant impact of conviction frameworks—aa power that shapes our impression of riches and, eventually, our monetary reality. In this fragment, we leave on a significant excursion of self-revelation, disentangling the complex snare of convictions that oversee our relationship with cash. Through contemplation and examination, perusers are welcome to go up against and challenge the profoundly imbued convictions that might be restricting their monetary potential. From adolescent molding to cultural standards, we investigate the sources from which these convictions start, engaging perusers to destroy the boundaries that block their way to success. Outfitted with newly discovered mindfulness, perusers are furnished with useful procedures for revamping their conviction frameworks, changing deliberate constraints into venturing stones for development. By developing a mentality established in probability and overflow, they tackle the groundbreaking force of conviction to show their monetary yearnings with steadfast clarity and conviction. Drawing upon the insight of brain research and self-improvement, this part fills in as a reference point for edification, directing perusers on a path of self-acknowledgment and strengthening. As they embrace the freeing truth that their convictions shape their predetermination, perusers open the keys to opening their maximum capacity, preparing for an existence of overflow and satisfaction.

Embracing a Development Outlook

In the mission for monetary achievement, embracing a development outlook arises as a crucial determinant of one's excursion towards flourishing. This section enlightens the groundbreaking force of embracing a development-situated viewpoint, welcoming perusers to set out on an excursion of ceaseless learning and personal growth. At its center, a development mentality involves an undaunted faith in the potential for development and improvement, even despite difficulties and mishaps. Drawing motivation from the spearheading work of clinicians like Ditty Dweck, perusers are acquainted with the central rules that support this change in perspective in thinking. Through impactful tales and down-to-earth experiences, perusers find the intrinsic strength that goes with a development mentality—aa flexibility that empowers them to explore misfortune with elegance and determination. By rethinking misfortunes as any open doors for learning and development, perusers rise above the impediments of a decent mentality, leaving a direction of endless potential. Furnished with systems for encouraging a development-situated mentality, perusers are enabled to develop propensities and ways of behaving that impel them towards their monetary objectives. From embracing disappointment as a venturing stone to progress to supporting an energy for long-lasting learning, every rule fills in as a signal of direction on the way to abundance dominance. As perusers incorporate the groundbreaking force of a development mentality, they leave on an excursion of self-disclosure and strengthening, ready to understand their fullest expected chasing monetary overflow. With each step in the right direction, they epitomize the embodiment of versatility, constancy, and boundless chance, establishing the groundwork for a future characterized by unmatched achievement and satisfaction.

Adjusting objectives to values

In the tangled scene of abundance creation, adjusting monetary objectives to profoundly held values arises as a reference point of lucidity—aa directing light enlightening the way to getting through flourishing. This section leaves on a significant investigation of the harmonious connection between private qualities and monetary desires, welcoming perusers to set out on an excursion of self-disclosure and arrangement. At its pith, the arrangement of objectives with values rises above simple monetary desire, enveloping an all-encompassing way to deal with abundance creation established in credibility and reason. Through contemplative activities and intelligent requests, perusers are urged to uncover the basic beliefs that act as the bedrock of their reality—values that pervade their monetary excursion with increasing importance. With newly discovered lucidity, perusers are engaged in creating a dream for their monetary future that reverberates profoundly with their characteristic qualities. By setting brilliant (explicit, quantifiable, feasible, persistent, and time-bound) objectives lined up with these qualities, they lay the foundation for a vital guide to abundance creation—one that respects their independence and cultivates a feeling of satisfaction enroute. As perusers leave on this extraordinary excursion of arrangement, they are directed by the rule that genuine abundance reaches out past material overflow, incorporating a feeling of direction, commitment, and satisfaction. By adjusting their monetary objectives to their most profound qualities, perusers open the way to an existence of significance, credibility, and overflow—aa daily existence where monetary achievement isn't only an objective but also an impression of their most genuine selves.

Developing Appreciation and Overflow

Chasing riches and flourishing, developing a demeanor of appreciation arises as an intense power—an impetus for opening the unfathomable overflow that penetrates each feature of our reality. This part digs into the groundbreaking force of appreciation, welcoming perusers to embrace its significant ramifications for their monetary excursion. At its center, appreciation fills in as a door to overflow—aa focal point through which we see the endless gifts that ease our lives every day. Through thoughtful activities and intelligent practices, perusers are urged to develop an outlook of appreciation, arousing the wealth that encompasses them in each second. As perusers dig further into the act of appreciation, they uncover its significant effect on their monetary reality. By moving their concentration from shortage to overflow, they rise above the impediments of a world view limited by fear, opening themselves to the boundless potential outcomes that have large amounts of the domain of abundance creation. Drawing upon the standards of positive brain science and care, perusers figure out how to bridle the groundbreaking force of appreciation in their day-to-day routines. From keeping an appreciation diary to rehearsing irregular thoughtful gestures, every method fills in as a venturing stone on the way to monetary overflow. As perusers embrace the act of developing appreciation, they witness firsthand its significant, gradually expanding influence on their monetary excursion. By recognizing and valuing the overflow that, as of now, exists inside and around them, they prepare for a future characterized by boundless success, satisfaction, and bliss.

{ 2 }

Chapter 2: Building Wealth from Within

Becoming the best at self-restraint

At the foundation of each and every effective monetary excursion lies the relentless mainstay of self-restraint—aa quality that isolates the visionaries from the achievers and the wannabes from the experts. In this part, we dive profoundly into the significant meaning of self-restraint in the domain of abundance creation, unwinding its extraordinary power in forming our monetary fate. Self-control fills in as the directing power that drives us forward on the way to monetary achievement, imparting inside us the purpose to remain consistent with our objectives and yearnings even notwithstanding misfortune. Through piercing bits of knowledge and pragmatic techniques, perusers are engaged to develop this significant quality, fashioning an immovable obligation to their drawn-out goals. From laying out clear and reachable monetary objectives to laying out schedules and frameworks that cultivate efficiency and concentration, perusers are furnished with a thorough toolbox for becoming the best at self-restraint. By saddling the impact of trained instinctive arrangement and resolve, they rise above the brief appeal of moment satisfaction, establishing the groundwork for reasonable abundance amassing. Also, this part offers direction on conquering normal traps, for example, delaying and driving spending, enabling perusers to continue through to the end in any event when the excursion becomes testing. By embracing inconvenience as an impetus for development and change, they epitomize the embodiment of self-control, arising as draftsmen of their monetary predetermination. As perusers incorporate the standards of self-control and coordinate them into their regular routines, they open the way to opening their maximum capacity, setting out on an excursion of unmatched development and flourishing. With each focused activity, they inch nearer to their monetary yearnings, invigorated by the steady determination that separates them as bosses of their destiny.

Monetary Education: The Groundwork of Abundance

In the mind-boggling embroidery of abundance creation, monetary proficiency arises as the foundation upon which enduring success is fabricated—an underpinning of information and understanding that enables people to explore the intricacies of individual accounting with certainty and discernment. This portion leaves on an excursion of edification, disentangling the fundamental ideas and rules that structure the bedrock of monetary education. At its core, monetary education encompasses a broadness of information incorporating planning, saving, effective money management, and obligation—abilities that are fundamental for achieving long-term monetary soundness and achievement. Through astute conversations and viable direction, perusers become acquainted with the central rules that support sound monetary navigation, outfitting them with the apparatuses they need to assume command over their monetary predetermination. From the nuts and bolts of making a family financial plan to the subtleties of speculation methodologies and retirement planning, this part offers a far-reaching outline of fundamental monetary ideas. Through illustrative models and genuine situations, perusers gain a more profound comprehension of how these ideas apply to their own lives, engaging them to settle on informed choices that line up with their monetary objectives and desires. Also, this section features the significance of progressing training and personal growth in the domain of individual budget, empowering perusers to ceaselessly extend their insight and abilities to adjust to changing monetary circumstances and market patterns. By embracing a deep-rooted obligation to learn, perusers position themselves for supported monetary achievement and security in a steadily developing scene. As perusers develop their monetary education and apply these standards to their own lives, they set out on an excursion of strengthening and self-revelation, ready to open the ways to independence from the rat race and overflow. With each recently discovered understanding, they inch nearer to their monetary objectives, sustained by the information and certainty that come from dominating the essentials of an individual budget.

Utilizing the Force of Perception

Chasing monetary overflow, the act of perception arises as a powerful instrument—aa passage to showing our most profound longings and goals with clarity and conviction. This segment digs into the extraordinary capability of perception, welcoming perusers to harness the force of their creative mind to speed up their excursion towards monetary achievement. Perception, at its center, includes making striking mental pictures of our ideal results, pervading them with feelings, and aiming to impel them into the real world. Through vivid activities and useful procedures, perusers are directed to take advantage of the boundless capability of their psyche, developing an unmistakable and convincing vision of their monetary future. By adjusting their contemplations, sentiments, and activities with their imagined results, perusers enact the all-inclusive guideline of indication, bringing riches and overflow into their lives effortlessly. From picturing the accomplishment of monetary objectives to epitomizing the feelings related to progress, every representation practice fills in as an impetus for change and development. Besides, this part investigates the significant association between perception and objective accomplishment, featuring the role of centered aim and faith in molding our world. By developing a feeling of enduring confidence in the fulfillment of their monetary goals, perusers open the keys to opening their maximum capacity, making ready for a future characterized by flourishing and overflow. As perusers incorporate representation into their day-to-day daily schedule, they set out on an excursion of self-revelation and strengthening, arousing the endless potential outcomes that exist in their grip. With every representation practice, they conform to the recurrence of riches and overflow, polarizing amazing open doors and assets to help their excursion towards independence from the rat race and satisfaction.

The general rule that good energy attracts good in abundance creation

At the nexus of quantum material science and transcendentalism lies a significant rule—aa widespread regulation known as the Pattern of Good Following Good—aa power that oversees the vibrational pith of our world and holds the way to opening endless overflow. This fragment digs into the magical domains of sign, welcoming perusers to bridle the extraordinary force of the pattern of energy, attracting similar energy in their quest for monetary flourishing. Fundamental to the pattern of good following good is the rule that like draws in like—that which we center our considerations, feelings, and expectations upon, we unavoidably bring into our lives. Through a mix of reflection and viable application, perusers are directed to adjust their inward world to their external reality, developing a condition of reverberation with their ideal monetary results. By tackling the imaginative influence of their viewpoints and convictions, perusers become cognizant co-makers of their monetary fate, imbuing their dreams of riches and overflow with unfaltering confidence and aim. From confirmations and perceptions to appreciation practices and demonstrations of liberality, each purposeful activity fills in as a powerful impetus for enacting the Pattern of Good Following Good and introducing a deluge of monetary overflow. Additionally, this segment investigates the job of vibrational arrangement in the sign cycle, stressing the significance of developing positive feelings and high-recurrence vibrations to easily draw in riches. By epitomizing the quintessence of overflow in their viewpoints, sentiments, and activities, perusers polarize valuable open doors and assets that help their excursion towards independence from the rat race and satisfaction. As perusers embrace the standards of the Pattern of Good Following Good and incorporate them into their day-to-day routines, they set out on an excursion of strengthening and self-acknowledgment, arousing the endless potential that dwells inside them. With each cognizant idea and purposeful activity, they conform to the recurrence of riches and overflow, introducing another time of thriving and plausibility in their lives.

Developing and Establishing Financial Stability Outlook

In the prolific soil of the brain, the seeds of abundance are planted, supported by the rich waters of expectation and conviction. This part dives into the extraordinary influence of developing a growing long-term financial stability outlook—aa mentality that fills in as the rich ground whereupon monetary overflow prospers and flourishes. At its pith, establishing a strong financial foundation mentality rises above simple material securing, enveloping a comprehensive way to deal with abundance creation that includes overflow in the entirety of its structures—monetary, profound, and otherworldly. Through thoughtful requests and functional direction, perusers are enabled to develop a mentality established in probability, overflow, and flourishing. Integral to this outlook is the development of engaging convictions and mentalities that help the fulfillment of monetary objectives. From beating the shortage attitude to embracing the boundless capability of overflow, perusers are directed to destroy the psychological hindrances that have upset their monetary development and open the entryways to success. In addition, this part investigates the role of propensities and ways of behaving in molding our monetary reality, accentuating the significance of embracing rehearsals that line up with our establishing long-term financial stability objectives. From trained saving and contributing to developing a mentality of appreciation and liberality, each propensity fills in as a structure block in the development of a strong starting point for enduring flourishing. As perusers coordinate the standards of establishing a long-term financial stability mentality into their regular routines, they set out on an excursion of self-revelation and strengthening, arousing the innate potential that lies lethargic inside them. With each purposeful idea and conscious activity, they plant the seeds of monetary overflow, sustaining them with unfaltering confidence and assurance until they bloom.

Chapter 3: Overcoming Obstacles to Wealth

Recognizing and Beating Monetary Barricades

Inside the maze of abundance creation lies a heap of detours and snags—challenges that, whenever left ignored, can crash even the most relentless monetary excursion. This part fills in as a signal of direction, enlightening the normal monetary road obstructions that substitute the way to abundance gathering and offering key answers for conquering them. Through reflection and investigation, perusers are engaged to distinguish the deterrents that might be preventing their monetary advancement, whether it be obligation, monetary uncertainty, or unforeseen mishaps. By revealing insight into these difficulties, perusers gain a newly discovered feeling of clarity and direction, laying the groundwork for groundbreaking activity. Outfitted with functional methodologies and instruments, perusers leave on an excursion of strengthening, furnishing themselves with the abilities and assets expected to conquer monetary obstructions with flexibility and elegance. From obligation decrease methods to planning and investment fund procedures, every arrangement fills in as a stepping stone on the way to independence from the rat race. Additionally, this part digs into the significance of building flexibility despite monetary mishaps and difficulty. By rethinking difficulties as any open doors for development and learning, perusers develop a mentality of strength, empowering them to explore deterrents with certainty and assurance. As perusers carry out these methodologies into their monetary lives, they emerge more grounded and stronger than at any other time, engaged to beat any hindrance that stands between them and their monetary objectives. With each challenge vanquished, they inch nearer to their vision of monetary overflow, strengthened by their resolute confidence in their capacity to beat affliction and flourish.

Overseeing Dread and Hazards in Financial Planning

In the domain of abundance creation, the phantom of dread poses a potential threat—aa considerable obstruction that takes steps to block our excursion towards monetary achievement. This part dives into the brain research of dread and its significant effect on venture choices, offering priceless experiences and methodologies for overseeing risk with certainty and clarity. Dread, frequently established in vulnerability and misgiving, can possibly deaden even the most prepared financial backers, keeping them from going ahead with carefully thought-out plans of action and immediately jumping all over rewarding chances. Through thoughtfulness and examination, perusers are welcome to stand up to their feelings of dread head-on, unwinding the basic convictions and feelings that fuel their nerves. Outfitted with a more profound comprehension of the mental elements at play, perusers are engaged to take on an objective and vital way to deal with overseeing risk in their speculation attempts. From broadening and resource designation to taking a chance with evaluation and relief methodologies, every procedure fills in as a defense against the tide of dread, empowering financial backers to explore tempestuous waters with certainty and balance. Besides, this part investigates the idea of dread of disappointment—an unavoidable trepidation that can undermine our monetary yearnings and keep us from understanding our maximum capacity. By reexamining disappointment as a characteristic and unavoidable piece of the venture cycle, perusers develop versatility and persistence, empowering them to return quickly from misfortunes with recharged assurance. As perusers execute these procedures into their venture approach, they emerge more grounded and stronger, invigorated by the information that they have the apparatuses and assets expected to explore vulnerability with beauty and certainty. With dread done holding them hostage, they leave on an excursion of monetary development and flourishing, directed by an unflinching confidence in their capacity to overcome difficulty and flourish.

Exploring Financial Vulnerability

In the wild scene of abundance creation, monetary vulnerability remains a considerable enemy—aa power fit for disturbing even the most painstakingly laid monetary plans. This segment fills in as a reference point of direction, offering priceless procedures for exploring the recurring patterns of financial unpredictability with strength and premonition. Monetary vulnerability is an unavoidable part of the monetary scene, portrayed by changes in business sectors, changes in buyer conduct, and international unsteadiness. Through smart investigation and key premonition, perusers are engaged to adjust to changing monetary circumstances and immediately jump all over chances for development and abundance creation. Vital to exploring monetary vulnerability is the capacity to stay spry and adaptable in one's monetary methodology. By broadening venture portfolios, keeping up with liquidity, and remaining informed about market patterns, perusers can situate themselves to face the hardships of monetary disturbance and arise more grounded on the opposite side. In addition, this segment investigates the significance of safeguarding abundance during times of vulnerability, underscoring the job of hazard management and monetary preparation in defending resources against likely slumps. From saving crisis assets to supporting market instability, every methodology fills in as a defense against the eccentric idea of financial variances. As perusers integrate these techniques into their monetary plans, they emerge more grounded and stronger despite financial vulnerability, furnished with the information and assets expected to explore violent waters with certainty and lucidity. With each challenge they survive, they inch nearer to their monetary objectives, strengthened by their faithful confidence in their capacity to flourish in any financial environment.

Conquering Self-Restricting Convictions

In the multifaceted embroidery of abundance creation, the most considerable snags frequently lie not in outer conditions but rather inside the bounds of our own personalities. This segment digs into the significant effect of self-restricting convictions on our monetary excursion, offering extraordinary experiences and methodologies for defeating these psychological hindrances with flexibility and assurance. Self-restricting convictions are profoundly instilled examples of beliefs that subvert our certainty, harm our endeavors, and frustrate our capacity to accomplish our monetary objectives. Whether established in youth encounters, cultural molding, or past disappointments, these convictions have a strong effect on our view of riches and achievement. Through contemplation and mindfulness, perusers are engaged to distinguish and challenge themselves, restricting convictions that might be keeping them from understanding their full monetary potential. By reevaluating negative considerations and convictions about cash, perusers can develop an outlook of overflow and plausibility, empowering them to break free from the shackles of self-uncertainty and weakness. Besides, this part investigates methods for building fearlessness and self-viability in the quest for abundance. From positive confirmations and perception activities to mental conduct treatment and outlook instructing, perusers are furnished with an exhaustive tool compartment for changing their mentality and modifying the story of their monetary future. As perusers defy and conquer their self-restricting convictions, they become more grounded and stronger, invigorated by the information that they have the ability to shape their own fate. With each restricting conviction destroyed, they inch nearer to their monetary objectives, pushed by a recently discovered feeling of strengthening and plausibility.

Creating a Steady Financial Momentum Organization

In the midst of the excursion towards monetary flourishing, the meaning of a steady organization couldn't possibly be more significant. This portion enlightens the urgent job of encircling oneself with strong and similar people in cultivating a helpful climate for abundance creation. A strong abundance network fills in as a foundation of progress, offering important direction, support, and responsibility along the way to monetary overflow. By developing associations with tutors, counselors, and friends who share a typical vision of thriving, perusers get close enough to an abundance of information and experience that can speed up their excursion towards their monetary objectives. Through coordinated effort and shared help, perusers are engaged to overcome difficulties and take advantage of chances for development and extension. Whether through system administration occasions, plan gatherings, or on-line networks, the force of aggregate insight and shared encounters fills in as an impetus for change and achievement. Besides, this part investigates the significant effect of local area and association on our mentality and conduct towards riches. By encircling ourselves with people who exemplify the standards of overflow and achievement, we are enlivened to increase our own expectations and take a stab at greatness in each part of our lives. As perusers develop their abundance organization, they become more grounded and stronger, strengthened by the help and fellowship of similar people who share their vision of monetary flourishing. With every association produced and relationship sustained, they inch nearer to their monetary objectives, moved by the aggregate energy and excitement of their strong local area.

{ 4 }

Chapter 4: Sustaining and Multiplying Wealth

The Significance of Monetary Discipline and Long-Haul Arranging

At the foundation of supported abundance gathering lies the relentless obligation to monetary discipline and fastidious long-haul arranging. This part fills in as a directing guide, enlightening the significant meaning of developing restrained monetary propensities and making smart plans that prepare for persevering through success. Monetary discipline isn't only a question of confining spending or sticking to a financial plan; rather, it is an outlook—an unfaltering obligation to judicious monetary stewardship and postponed delight. Through quick conversations and reasonable direction, perusers are engaged to embrace restrained monetary propensities, making way for a future characterized by monetary security and overflow. Besides, this part digs into the groundbreaking force of long-haul arranging—an interaction that includes imagining one's monetary objectives and making a guide to accomplishing them. From retirement wanting to abundance safeguarding techniques, perusers are directed to contemplate their monetary future, considering elements like expansion, market instability, and the future. By developing trained monetary propensities and embracing long-haul arrangements, perusers lay the foundation for supported abundance aggregation and independence from the rat race. With each purposeful choice and vital activity, they inch nearer to their monetary objectives, sustained by the information that their persevering endeavors today will make ready for a more splendid tomorrow.

Speculation Procedures for Abundance, Safeguarding, and Development

In the unique scene of abundance on the board, key venture choices assume an essential role in both safeguarding existing riches and cultivating their development. This fragment digs into the complexities of speculation procedures, offering important experiences and functional strategies for exploring the intricacies of the monetary business sectors with certainty and reasonability. Fundamental to compelling abundance on the board is the investigation of assorted venture roads that take care of both abundance protection and development targets. From conventional resources, for example, stocks and bonds, to elective ventures like land and wares, perusers are acquainted with a range of choices intended to suit their extraordinary gamble resistance and monetary objectives. In addition, this part digs into the significance of the executives strategies for shielding ventures against market unpredictability and unanticipated occasions. Through expansion, resource allotment, and supporting methodologies, perusers figure out how to moderate possible misfortunes while expanding returns, accordingly upgrading their speculation portfolios for long-haul achievement. By taking on a key and differentiated way to deal with financial planning, perusers position themselves to endure the hardships of monetary vulnerability and exploit valuable open doors for abundance creation. With each educated choice and reasonable assignment regarding assets, they inch nearer to their monetary goals, braced by the information that their speculations are working perseveringly to get their monetary future.

Bequest Arranging and Abundance Move

In the complicated embroidery of abundance on the board, the significance of domain arranging couldn't possibly be more significant—aa basic part of guaranteeing the consistent exchange of resources and the safeguarding of one's monetary heritage for people in the future. This part digs into the subtleties of domain arranging, offering vital experiences and down-to-earth strategies for exploring this intricate landscape with lucidity and premonition. At its essence, home arranging includes the smart use of one's resources and issues to work with their exchange with expected recipients in a way that limits charges, dodges probate, and ensures abundance for people in the future. Through savvy conversations and master direction, perusers are engaged to make extensive bequest designs that mirror their qualities, needs, and goals. From wills and trusts to legal authorities and medical services mandates, perusers gain a more profound comprehension of the fundamental parts of a powerful domain plan and the significance of occasional surveys and updates to guarantee its pertinence and viability over the long haul. Also, this part investigates progressed bequest arranging systems, for example, giving, altruistic giving, and the utilization of extra security, to expand charge productivity and streamline abundance move results. By proactively tending to home-arranging contemplations, perusers defend their monetary heritage and engage their friends and family to explore the intricacies of abundance with certainty and inner serenity. With each purposeful choice and vital activity, they prepare for a consistent progress of resources and an enduring heritage that rises above ages.

Magnanimity and Offering in Return

In the midst of the quest for monetary success lies a significant chance for generosity—an opportunity to persevere through effect and leave a legacy that stretches out a long way past simple abundance collection. This section digs into the extraordinary influence of generosity, offering experiences and techniques for integrating beneficent surrendering to one's abundance. The executives plan with aim and reason. Charity isn't just a demonstration of liberality; it is an essential interest in the improvement of society—aa cognizant choice to use one's assets for everyone's benefit. Through thoughtfulness and reflection, perusers are welcome to investigate their qualities, interests, and areas of premium, distinguishing causes and associations that resound profoundly with their generous vision. Besides, this part dives into the different ways in which people can participate in generosity, from direct gifts to magnanimous trusts, benefactor-exhorted reserves, and arranged giving methodologies. By utilizing charge-proficient giving vehicles and investigating imaginative ways to deal with altruism, perusers can boost the effect of their altruistic commitments and make enduring change in their networks, among other things. Past the unmistakable advantages of generosity lies a significant feeling of satisfaction and reason—an acknowledgment that genuine abundance stretches beyond material belongings to the lives we contact and the distinctions we make on the planet. As perusers embrace the groundbreaking influence of charity, they set out on an excursion of self-improvement and social effect, leaving a heritage that rises above monetary riches and perseveres for a long time into the future.

Ceaseless learning and transformation

In the unique scene of abundance among the executives, there is one steady remaining part: the basic of constant learning and transformation. This segment highlights the essential job of progressing schooling and variation in supporting and duplicating abundance over the long haul. As monetary scenes advance and monetary business sectors vary, remaining educated and side by side with the latest things and improvements is central. Through a promise to deep-rooted learning, perusers outfit themselves with the information and bits of knowledge expected to explore changing financial circumstances and jump all over chances for development and extension. In addition, this part investigates techniques for remaining informed about monetary patterns and speculation, from keeping up to date with monetary news and market examinations to drawing in with industry specialists and thought pioneers. By staying cautious and proactive in their way to deal with learning, perusers position themselves to exploit arising patterns and creative ventures that open doors. As well as remaining informed, flexibility is key in the steadily impacting universe of abundance. By embracing advancement and adaptability, perusers can turn and change their monetary methodologies in light of moving business sector elements and financial circumstances, guaranteeing that their abundance stays tough and versatile notwithstanding vulnerability. As perusers embrace the standards of consistent learning and variation, they emerge more grounded and stronger, braced by the information and experiences expected to explore the intricacies of abundance with certainty and lucidity. With each new example learned and key change made, they inch nearer to their monetary objectives, enabled by their relentless obligation to development and achievement.

{ 5 }

Chapter 5: Conclusion and Action Plan

Recap of Key Ideas and Experiences

As we finish up our excursion through the pages of this book, it is fundamental to ponder the crucial ideas and significant experiences that have formed how we might interpret abundance creation. In this part, we return to the vital subjects and standards examined all through our investigation, supporting their importance after monetary achievement. We start by summing up the principal ideas that support the mogul outlook—underscoring the extraordinary force of attitude, discipline, and vital preparation in establishing the groundwork for persevering through thriving. By developing a mentality of overflow, embracing trained monetary propensities, and creating brilliant courses of action lined up with our drawn-out objectives, we set ourselves on a direction towards monetary overflow and satisfaction. Additionally, we dig into the excursion from attitude change to noteworthy stages, featuring the significance of making an interpretation of our newly discovered bits of knowledge into substantial methodologies and ways of behaving. From laying out Savvy objectives to executing viable, long-term financial stability procedures, each step is a demonstration of our obligation to take responsibility for the monetary future and chart a course towards thriving. As we think about the vital ideas and experiences examined all through this book, we are helped to remember the significant possibility that exists in every one of us to make the existence of overflow and satisfaction we want possible. By incorporating these standards and resolving to activity, we prepare for a future characterized by independence from the rat race, thriving, and satisfaction.

Making Your Customized Activity Plan

Since we have acquired a complete comprehension of the standards and procedures for abundance creation, the time has come to make an interpretation of our recently discovered information into significant stages. In this segment, we set out on the excursion of creating a customized activity plan custom-made to our individual monetary objectives and goals. We start by setting clear and explicit goals and recognizing what we expect to accomplish in the short, medium, and long haul. Whether it's accomplishing a specific degree of reserve funds, taking care of obligations, or putting resources into pay-producing resources, articulating our objectives with accuracy is the most important move towards transforming our fantasies into the real world. Then, we separate our objectives into sensible activity steps, outlining the particular assignments and achievements that will push us towards progress. By stalling our objectives into scaled-down increases, we create a guide that is both noteworthy and feasible, enabling us to gain consistent headway towards our ideal results. Besides, we distinguish the assets and emotionally supportive networks expected to execute our activity plan successfully. Whether it's utilizing monetary instruments and innovations, looking for direction from coaches and counsels, or enrolling the help of responsibility accomplices, encircling ourselves with the right assets guarantees that we have the vital help to keep focused and conquer difficulties enroute. As we make our customized activity plan, we perceive that adaptability and flexibility are fundamental elements of progress. While our objectives might stay steady, the way to accomplish them might develop as we experience new opportunities and difficulties. By staying open to changes and course adjustments, we guarantee that our activity plan stays pertinent and receptive to evolving conditions. In creating our customized activity plan, we take responsibility for our monetary future and focus on doing whatever it may take to transform our yearnings into accomplishments. With a reasonable guide close by, we leave on the excursion towards monetary accomplishment with certainty, assurance, and an unfaltering obligation to understand our fantasies.

Executing Procedures for Practical Abundance Creation

With our customized activity plan close by, we are prepared to leave on the excursion towards economic abundance creation. In this segment, we dive into the viable procedures and methods that will empower us to carry out our arrangement really, guaranteeing that we remain on track towards our monetary objectives. We start by incorporating the standards of abundance creation that we have advanced all through this book. Whether it's embracing focused saving and ways of managing money, differentiating our venture portfolio, or boosting our procuring potential through essential profession decisions or pioneering tries, every system assumes an imperative part as we continue looking for monetary achievement. In addition, we underline the significance of consistency and persistence in carrying out our long-term financial stability procedures. Rome was not an inherent day, nor are riches. By remaining focused on our arrangement and gaining steady headway every day, we progressively draw nearer to our objectives and gather speed that pushes us towards progress. Moreover, we influence the forces of robotization and innovation to smooth out our monetary administration processes and guarantee that we keep focused on our arrangement. Whether it's setting up programmed commitments to our reserve funds and speculation accounts, utilizing planning applications to follow our costs, or utilizing robo-counselors to deal with our venture portfolios, innovation offers an abundance of instruments and assets to help our excursion towards independence from the rat race. As we execute our systems for maintainable abundance creation, we stay aware of the significance of adjusting to changing conditions and immediately jumping all over chances as they emerge. The way to monetary achievement isn't generally smooth, and startling difficulties might test our purpose enroute. Notwithstanding, by staying adaptable and versatile even with affliction, we show our obligation to accomplishing our objectives and understanding our fantasies. By executing these techniques for feasible abundance creation, we set before ourselves a way towards monetary freedom, security, and overflow. With each step in the right direction, we inch closer to the existence of opportunity and satisfaction that we imagine for ourselves as well as our friends and family.

Developing a Development Outlook for Proceeded with Progress

As we explore the intricacies of abundance creation, it is fundamental to develop a development outlook—aa mentality described by flexibility, versatility, and a pledge to consistent learning and improvement. In this segment, we investigate the groundbreaking force of a development outlook and its significant effect on our excursion towards monetary achievement. A development mentality is established in the conviction that our capacities and knowledge are not fixed yet but can be created through exertion, persistence, and gaining from disappointment. By embracing difficulties as any open doors for development, we open our maximum capacity and defeat obstructions sincerely and with flexibility. Besides, we perceive the significance of keeping an uplifting perspective and re-evaluating difficulties as important growth opportunities. Rather than survey disappointments as difficult barriers, we view them as venturing stones on the way to progress—chances to learn, develop, and advance into our best selves. Besides, we embrace the standards of flexibility and development, perceiving that the universe of abundance and creation is continually advancing. By remaining inquisitive and liberal, we stay light-footed in our methodology, prepared to turn and change our techniques because of changing business sector elements and financial circumstances. As we develop a development mentality, we invest in long-lasting learning and self-awareness. Whether it's remaining informed about arising patterns and advances, searching out tutors and counsels who can offer direction and backing, or putting resources into our own schooling and expertise improvement, we perceive that development is an excursion that goes on and on forever. By embracing a development mentality, we position ourselves to proceed with progress and accomplishment on our excursion towards independence from the rat race and satisfaction. With each new test embraced and example learned, we inch nearer to our objectives, enabled by our faith in our capacity to beat affliction and accomplish significance.

Resolving to Activity and Proceeding with Development

As we gravitate toward the end of our excursion towards monetary strengthening, reaffirming our obligation to make a move and seeking to proceed with growth is basic. In this last segment, we concrete our purpose to make an interpretation of our yearnings into the real world and to develop an existence of overflow and satisfaction. We start by genuinely committing to ourselves and our monetary objectives. We recognize that achieving riches and independence from the rat race requires something other than sincere goals—it requires unfaltering devotion, steadiness, and an eagerness to make a conclusive move, even despite vulnerability and misfortune. Besides, we perceive the significance of responsibility in our excursion towards monetary achievement. By imparting our objectives to confided-in companions, relatives, or tutors, we create an emotionally supportive network that holds us to our responsibilities and gives consolation and direction enroute. Besides, we embrace the standard of proceeding with development and advancement, perceiving that the quest for abundance isn't simply an objective yet a long-lasting excursion. We stay open to new doors, new difficulties, and better approaches to thinking, realizing that each experience can possibly grow our viewpoints and improve our lives. As we resolve to engage in activity and proceed with development, we embrace the innate potential inside us to create the overflow and satisfaction we want. With each step in the right direction, we reaffirm our faith in our capacity to defeat impediments, immediately jump all over chances, and eventually, to accomplish our monetary dreams. All things being equal, let us set out on this excursion with boldness, assurance, and a relentless obligation to understand our maximum capacity. Together, we will outline a course towards independence from the rat race and make a tradition of success that perseveres for a long time into the future.